AMERICA UNDER FIRE

AMERICA UNDER FIRE

3 Things America Must Do to
Rebuild its Foundation

Jim Romeo

To order additional copies of this book, contact:
Xlibris
1-888-795-4274
www.Xlibris.com
Orders@Xlibris.com

CONTENTS

1. Introduction (Thinking Outside the Box) 1

2. America Must Learn How to Fight a Guerrilla War 3

3. An Economic Solution That No One Thought Of 17

4. The Other Side of Racism (It's Embarrassing Being White, and It's Not All Right to Be Lily-White) 29

5. Conclusion 53

INTRODUCTION
(THINKING OUTSIDE THE BOX)

THE PURPOSE OF THIS BOOK is to hopefully open people's eyes and make them aware that there are other ways of looking at things. We, in America, as well as the rest of the world, seem to be locked into doing things the same old way even if it's obvious that it doesn't work that well. First, I'll give a different solution to the impotent way America always insists upon fighting a guerrilla war. Many of the same mistakes we made in Vietnam where making again in Iraq and Afghanistan. Why? Second, I know very little about the economy, but I've come up with an economic solution I think we have to start to consider. I know this solution will probably never be implemented, but I think people in this country have to start thinking in this direction or our economic problems will eventually snowball out of control for good. Third, racism in this country, I feel, is the foundation of all our social and cultural problems. It seems to handcuff our nation in its ability to deal with our internal problems. I feel that we (especially white people) have to start seeing that there's another side to racism and stop believing all the propaganda our brains have been bombarded with by the media since we've been born. Believe me, if you've never been in a bad racial situation, you don't know anything about racism. And almost all the lily-white people in the media never had to live through any bad racial situations, so what would they really know about racism? The answer is very little, if anything at all.

AMERICA MUST LEARN HOW TO FIGHT A GUERRILLA WAR

TO INTRODUCE MYSELF, I HAVE a master's degree in geophysics, and I'm presently working as a third officer or in the crew in the United States Merchant Marine. Why? Because I find working a regular eight-to-five job in America makes life itself much too boring. However, I believe this story really starts in August of 1972. I just graduated from high school and joined the United States Marine Corps so I could go to Vietnam and help out in the war effort. Five and a half months later, in January of 1973, I completed my training, and soon after that, we were called on standby twice for a possible deployment to Vietnam. At this time, we were bombing the hell out of North Vietnam to, in effect, bring them to their knees at the bargaining tables in Paris, at the peace talks. Well, it worked. President Nixon finally took off the gloves and hurt them; he started bombing real targets in North Vietnam (Hanoi, Haiphong Harbor, etc.). Now the leaders of North Vietnam were no longer protected by American rules and regulations. A few months later, in May of 1973, North Vietnam signed the Paris peace agreement. True in a way, it wasn't much of an accomplishment as the lines drawn on the maps were gray and sketchy, and two years after all American ground forces left Vietnam, in April of 1975, North Vietnam launched a full-scale invasion of South Vietnam. At this time, South Vietnam waited, and as soon as they saw that America wasn't going to come back and fight their war again, they surrendered without firing a shot. Why? Because American ideals (the right to vote, being successful, etc.) were of little importance to them; they had their own culture, and that's what they wanted. Why am I mentioning this? Because I think America is making the same mistakes again in Iraq and Afghanistan? History repeats itself; that's the greatest thing I think we can learn from it. Yet no one seems to be learning. Vietnam, like Iraq and Afghanistan, also had some sound reasoning and logic for America's original involvement. If you remember, the people running the country back then were mostly WWII veterans. They had suffered more than probably anyone reading this book can ever understand. It was generally agreed upon back then by everyone that if the world stopped Hitler much earlier, the horror of WWII would have been much, much less. So there was some sound logic in our original involvement dealing with Russia's expansion. After all, Stalin was reported to have killed more of his own people during and after the war than Hitler did, and after Vietnam fell, so did Cambodia. When the communists took over in Cambodia, I believe one-third of their people, millions of people, were murdered by the Khmer Rouge. Yet the world completely ignored this. At the time, I would find small paragraphs in American newspapers, on usually next to the last page, on Cambodia. The newspapers, which mostly supported the cowards of the peace movement during the Vietnam War, didn't want to acknowledge that the cowards they supported could have been wrong. However, the main problem of the Vietnam War came when American politicians, admirals, and generals in the military were unable to adjust to fighting a guerrilla war. They made a simple task an impossible one, and the cowards in the peace movement in America compounded the problem by becoming one of North Vietnam's greatest allies. This is the first time in American history that an entire generation of Americans spit on the American military and ran from a confrontation. However, the first part of this book is about the war on terror, so why am I talking about Vietnam? Because in many ways we're making the same mistakes all over again. Remember, history usually repeats itself!

So how do you fight and win a guerrilla war? Well, there's only two ways to do it. First is the way America usually tries to fight and win a guerrilla war. This could work in some situations but will almost always fail if America tries this strategy. Why? Because the people we're fighting for have no interest in what we're trying to give them, and in general, the world is rooting against us. However, I must admit there is some sound logic to it, but what's scary is the fact that our country can't seem to adjust when it's obvious that it's not working. We used this strategy in Vietnam, and we're using it again in Iraq and Afghanistan. We go in and win the war militarily and then insist upon setting up a Western-type government (the right to vote and all that baloney). Well, it sounds good and it is a good idea, but that's where we fall flat on our faces every time. I'm an officer in the merchant marine. I've been to the Middle East and

Persian Gulf region many times. It's a nice place in general, but the people over there have absolutely *no* interest in what America calls democracy. Yes, they want freedom and democracy, but not connected to or organized by a Western government. They have their own culture, and that's what they want. America can't seem to understand this. We seem to think that if we give them the right to vote and throw a lot of money at them, they're going to love us. Well, it doesn't work that way. The governments we create usually grab all the money, leaving the everyday people, the ones we must reach, with nothing. These people, which we must reach, usually end up despising us. See if you're fighting a guerrilla war, this only works if the people you're fighting for take up your cause because they think that what you're offering them is a cause they want. It doesn't work if the people don't have any interest in what you're offering them or despise the government you created to help them, even if it is better. In Iraq and Afghanistan, after we won the war, we should have stayed a maximum of six months. By this time, it was evident that the local people there weren't interested enough in what we were offering them for us to stay any longer. The Afghan people have always been known to be very good fighters. And here it is ten years later, and we still can't leave because they still haven't been properly trained. Dah! It didn't take ten years to train the Taliban, so obviously the local people in Afghanistan aren't really interested in what we're offering. That's OK. It's no big deal. President Bush, should have just got on the news one night and stated the war's over, we're leaving. They just weren't really interested in our help in setting up a new government, so we're leaving. We'll still continue to hunt terrorists in that country and any other country that harbors them, and we'll go back into Iraq or Afghanistan anytime they pose a threat to us. American politicians in general can't seem to understand this. They still insist upon setting up a government, have the people vote on it, and then sit back thinking they did some good, and then can't understand what's still going wrong. Well, what's going wrong in Iraq and Afghanistan is that the people over there consider us to be foreigners and, in general, have *no* interest in a Western-type government and don't trust or feel comfortable with the government we created. They're *not* taking up the cause and fighting hard for what we call democracy. In general, they probably have *no* interest in what we call democracy. In fact, over the years, we probably lost their respect more than we gained their trust. Vietnam, Iraq, Afghanistan—all these little piss-ass countries have embarrassed us by making us look impotent because the make-believe governments we create soon collapse after our military leaves.

So what should America do every time it gets bogged down in a guerrilla war? Well, the second way to fight a guerrilla war and the way America must fight this war is to become the guerrilla. An example of this and how effective it would be is how President Reagan handled the war in Libya. Remember that short ten-minute war? Libya's President Muammar Gadhafi was behind terror attacks and terror organizations for years, much like Osama bin Laden recently was. President Reagan finally said enough, and in about ten short minutes, he dropped a couple of tons of high explosives and left. *The secret to his success in this operation was that he left!* We never heard from Libya again, and the whole world loved us. If he, President Reagan, made the mistake of sending ten thousand marines into Libya after the attack, a few years later, three hundred thousand soldiers and marines would have been bogged down in a guerrilla war, and the whole world would have turned against us and hated us. People in America and around the world would have sided with our enemies and cheered at America's impotence in another third world country like Vietnam. A second example of America fighting a war the correct way was the First Persian Gulf War. After President Bush Senior retook Kuwait and accomplished his objectives, *which he kept simple and straightforward (extremely important), he left!* He never allowed it to become a guerrilla war. If he remained in the area to try to be everyone's friend and try to establish a Western-type government (well, just look at what happened with the Second Persian Gulf War), you figure it out. So, ladies and gentlemen, it's really an easy adjustment, and if our military could make this simple adjustment, our enemies wouldn't have a chance. The first thing necessary is for politicians, and maybe America in general, to stop thinking that these people we're fighting for actually want us there; or that they have something to gain (democracy, a friendly nation that has our interest at heart, the right to vote, women's rights, education for all children, oil, etc.). Yes, these all seem like good reasons, but it should be obvious by now to even politicians that the people in Iraq and Afghanistan aren't really interested, or we don't really know how to do this effectively. So the first thing we must do is to not care about all that. We gave it a shot; they didn't want it. Let's work with Afghanistan where the war is going. Pretty much pull all American troops out of the country, except possibly a few bases in very remote areas, some advisors, and some diplomatic people. After this, the Taliban would mass in a large force to attack the present government and probably get the best of them. At this point, we would know where they are, and they wouldn't know where we were. *We now have become the guerrilla force,* and with our military and all its technology, they wouldn't have a chance. Remember the beginning of the war? This would be similar. Back then we knew where the Taliban were, and they didn't know where we were. We went through them like a sharp knife going through hot butter. Again at this point, pretty much leave the country except for a few very minor things, maybe some military advisors and some minor diplomat-type people. If the Taliban attacked again (good) so what, let them. They'll again have to form in masses to topple the government we left behind. Once again we'll know where they are, and they won't know where we are. At this point, we'll once again be the guerrilla force, and they wouldn't have a chance. We could also attack them whenever we want as a guerrilla force or a conventional force, making sure that after the attack, *we left.* With our high-tech military, they wouldn't know what hit them. Isn't this what President Clinton did in Bosnia and President Obama did in Libya? Yes, ladies and gentlemen, this is exactly what happened. In Bosnia, President Clinton ordered the American military to use our high-tech military to bomb all targets, which were engaged in fighting the war. At this point, we became a guerrilla force! We used our high tech to bomb any target we wanted to bomb from far off. The Serbs were unable to shoot back; we were just too far away (maybe ten thousand to thirty thousand feet up in the sky). We were now fighting as a guerrilla force. We could kill and destroy them any time we wanted, and they didn't have the ability to shoot back. Well, the fighting stopped. You know it's no fun getting into a gunfight without a gun. Well, the war stopped. The Serbs couldn't shoot back at their invisible enemy in the sky. They didn't know where we were or when we would strike. We became a guerrilla force!

The recent situation in Libya was similar. The US and NATO used its high-tech military to bomb Gaddafi from afar. Gaddafi was unable to shoot back, paving a road for a rebel victory. Once again, America fought this war as a guerrilla force. We were able to kill and destroy them at any time. They didn't know where we were or when we would strike. We where a guerrilla force! If President Obama sent marines or soldiers into Libya, *big mistake!*

Isn't this what the American military complained about in Vietnam? We didn't know where the Vietcong were or when they would strike. Well, *dah!* If the uneducated Vietcong could do this, why can't the American military figure out this simple tactic? It seems we use it at times we're just not aware of it. You know you can be a high-tech guerrilla force. You don't have to live in a cave and eat nothing but rice for years to be a guerrilla force. A high-tech guerrilla force is much more effective than a low-tech guerrilla force! And of course, we can be a very effective low-tech guerrilla force if we need to be. Send our military in, whether it's land, sea, or air, small forces or large conventional forces using hit-and-run tactics. Even the beginning of the Iraq and Afghanistan wars could have fit into this category. You can send in hundreds of thousands of troops and go all the way to Baghdad or Kabul as a conventional force, but then after you get there, *leave!* Now the conventional force becomes a guerrilla force. Our enemies know that we can hit them like this at any time from the air, land, or sea with small forces or large conventional forces. By staying in Iraq and Afghanistan, we allowed our enemies to become the guerrilla force. Picking off Americans one at a time, they know where we are, and we don't know where they are, an extremely expensive war we can't afford, and a demoralizing war for the American military and the American people. And the worst might be yet to come, as Iraq as well as Afghanistan will probably become another South Vietnam (remember, history usually repeats itself). Even if we stay there for another ten or twenty years, shortly after we leave, whatever's going to happen is going to happen. Our continued presence there will probably have little effect on the outcome.

Probably the only way that our continued presence in places like Iraq and Afghanistan may be beneficial to us and them is to try to make improvements by making important ties with the people in the cities and country by helping them in ways that are meaningful to them. Building schools for both boys and girls so they all have a basic education. Provide medical clinics throughout the country so their people have at least some chance of seeing a doctor if it's necessary. Build orphanages with schools for all the orphans in the country produced by the war. Things like this would educate and help the people in a way they could and would understand. Then they would start to think of America in a positive way and get away from the stupidity of Islamic extremism. These days, usually the only schools available to their children are the madrasahs built by the Saudis, which from what I heard, are brainwashing centers for children in Islamic extremism and are main recruiting stations for the Taliban. Of course, if it's obvious that this isn't working, then just leave! It's no big deal. Hey, it didn't work; they weren't interested, so just leave altogether. We tried it; they weren't interested. Bye! If they are interested, *what about the cost!* Believe me, I don't want these countries to become another American welfare state—we already have too much of that. But we could probably do this for about 5 percent of what it cost us to fight the war with much better results. *As a reference, read the book Three Cups of Tea* by Greg Mortenson. Greg claims that it only costs one dollar a day to pay a teacher's salary in Pakistan, and I believe Afghanistan also, and I believe he builds most of his schools for about ten thousand dollars. He lets the local people supply the land and labor. We could probably afford that! Much cheaper than the cost of the war today! Of course, if American politicians got involved, the cost would probably increase one hundredfold. We constantly make things too complicated. When I went to school, I took a year and a half of calculus and a course in differential equations. Differential equations is a very hard branch of mathematics, and few people understand them in any way, shape, or form. In fact, most differential equations are unsolvable. The good news is that except for research, you'll probably never see them again. In the real world of science and engineering, usually all you have to do is add or subtract, multiply or divide with a little algebra and trigonometry now and then. The politicians in Washington are constantly making things more complicated than they need to be. Quit trying to solve differential equations when all you have to do is add and subtract. I love America and think that it's probably the greatest country in the world. However, America's got to learn how to keep its big nose out of everybody else's business. Why is it that the whole world seems to hate us? No one seems to hate Canada, Peru, Brazil, or Oman, but America seems to be the country everyone loves to hate, and people everywhere love it when we get bogged down in a guerrilla war just so they can laugh at our impotence. I believe America probably gives out more foreign aid than the rest of the countries in the world combined. So why does the rest of the world love to hate us? I don't know for sure, but I believe it's because we always stick our nose in everyone else's business. It must be due to politicians or big business or something stupid like that. Well, ladies and gentlemen, I suggest we strive to become a neutral nation like Switzerland. Of course, this couldn't be done overnight due to the stupid way we've behaved in the past, but in about ten or twenty years, this may be possible if we started to work on it now. Just trade with the rest of the world in a fair and open manner and quit sticking our noses in their business. Furthermore, we should refuse to get involved in their business. Didn't President Bush at first refuse to get involved in the Palestinian-Israeli problem? Didn't the world cry and scream that America had to get involved? Yeah, that went well. Now look at how they all love us. We should have refused to get involved. They have to solve their own problems; we certainly don't know how to do this, and every time we try, we fall flat on our own faces and the world laughs at us. So why keep on doing this? Isn't this what the old Monroe Doctrine of the early eighteen hundreds commanded our nation to do—*not* get involved with the rest of the world's problems? The founding fathers must have known something. Why did we get rid of this doctrine? If we can do this, I believe we would once again be the richest nation in the world.

Now I know, ladies and gentlemen, what I wrote doesn't apply precisely to every situation. However, I think America (especially politicians and generals) must start thinking like this. In a guerrilla war, if the people we're allied with don't take up our cause and fight hard (South Vietnam, Iraq, Afghanistan), fine, who cares! Just kick the crap out of who we're fighting and leave! You can't care about anything else. Our main concern is to knock the crap out of our enemies and leave. When they rally again, do what has to be done again, and leave again. In between these rallies, we can hit them hard anytime with small or large forces on the ground, air, or sea, and then leave (especially if we use ground forces, leave). There's nothing for America to win in a guerrilla war! If we try to win, we'll lose; if we don't try to win, we'll win. A famous general once wrote, "In a guerrilla war, if a conventional army tries to win, it will lose, and if a guerrilla army doesn't quit, it will win." America needs to understand this saying and act accordingly.

To try to sum this up, so everyone understands the point I'm trying to make. Our military must start using and always think about using guerrilla tactics in different conflicts. The four examples I gave are excellent. President Reagan's conflict in Libya, President Bush Senior in the 1st Persian Gulf War, President Clinton in Bosnia, and President Obama in Libya. I believe these tactics could be used effectively almost 100 percent of the time. On the few occasions when we actually have to topple a government, yes stay behind and try to help them rebuild there country and government. However, after about 6 months, if it's obvious that it's not working because they really don't want us there, just leave. Just say hey, we tried to help them rebuild there government and military, they really didn't want our help, that's OK it's there country if they would rather do it on there own that's fine, bye. We need to learn how to start thinking outside the *box!* Why are we having so much trouble with this?

AN ECONOMIC SOLUTION THAT NO ONE THOUGHT OF

ONCE AGAIN, I LOVE THIS country and think it's probably the greatest country in the world, but that doesn't mean that there's not alot of room for improvement. The economy, health care, alimony—Americans have become a nation of slaves. Why? Freedom, democracy, the right to vote, and all the rest of the great things that help make this nation great are still there, so what went wrong? Most Americans have become slaves to their jobs, "the stupidity of making money," that's what went wrong. Remember the Bible calls "love of money the root of all evil." Could God have been right? I don't know. You decide. Most Americans today, have no time to do anything anymore with their lives; that's what went wrong. We get up at 6:00 a.m., if not earlier (that's when your job really starts—when you get out of bed to go to work) you go to work, and you're lucky if you get home at 6:00 p.m. That's a twelve-hour day, ladies and gentlemen, not an eight-hour day, and lots of people work even more. Then you get home at this point most people only have the energy to eat a big meal and fall down on the couch, watch TV, or look at a magazine for a few hours, go to sleep just to get up in a few hours, and do it again. Sound familiar? That's what life's become in America for the majority of our people. Probably at least 96 percent of Americans have fallen into this thankless, endless misery that is our life in America today. That's not life, ladies and gentlemen. If anything, that's the complete absence of life. In many ways, we've become a nation of slaves. Considering most people in America probably only make enough money to pay the bills and get by (room, board, etc.); slaves pretty much had the same things (room, board, and a few extras). How can that be? This is America, and what can we do about it? Well, in Europe, I believe they start with four to six weeks vacation a year and then work their way up to eight weeks. I think eight weeks vacation a year should be mandatory, at least then, people would still have the time to enjoy their lives again. Something most people in America haven't done since they got out of school. I realize that in present-day America, this would be close to impossible due to the way everything's been run for so long, but it should be a goal we should strive for in the future, and maybe in about ten or twenty years, it could be attainable. Keeping the present system of one or two weeks off every year is just not acceptable. People in America are presently living to work, not working to live; their whole lives are completely consumed and controlled by their jobs. I realize that for some people and from the different jobs I've had. I would guess about less than 5 percent actually enjoy going to work every day, but for the majority of Americans, going to work every day is pure misery. Something that can be done right away, that could and would actually give Americans some of their freedom back, and make it possible for them to start enjoying their lives again, would be a four-day work week. Four ten-hour days instead of five eight-hour days! Think about it. Your day's usually shot anyway. If you get up at 6:00 a.m. and come home at 6:00 p.m., so you might as well stay two more hours. A few of my friends worked for companies that did this, and they all loved it. A three-day weekend is a huge difference. You actually have time to do things and enjoy your life again. Productivity might even go up just because people might actually start enjoying their lives once again, and going to work would no longer be such misery. A big problem with doing this might end up being with people themselves, in general, people are usually scared to try something different, even if they're miserable, they're comfortable in their misery. However, I feel that a four-day work week is mandatory for America to become America again. Without this, most Americans' lives will remain more miserable than happy. They will have no time to enjoy the freedoms that this country has to offer. This is also causing many Americans to become obese and develop health problems since all most Americans have the energy to do when they get home from work is eat a big meal (usually the high point of their day) and then fall down on the couch just to get up a few hours later and go to sleep. You remember land of the free, democracy, and all the good stuff that our nation was built upon? Well, "the stupidity of making money" has destroyed much of that. Americans seem to obsess with having everything (keeping up with the Joneses, I believe it was called when I was growing up). Well, now we all have the best toys but no time to play with them. How stupid!

So how do we get off this insane cycle that we're on? Well,

it won't be easy. This cancer has been building for such a long time, but it is doable. Many people at first may disagree with my proposal, but I believe the logic is sound. It may even be a form of socialism, I don't know nor do I care. I'm a geophysicist, not a politician (thank God), but I think it's the only way to solve all Americas economic problems including health care. Funny it's probably the only thing the politicians never discussed in all their stupid debates on health care. I actually did hear it mentioned on the news (Fox or CNN) once or twice (they talked about lowering salaries in the medical profession), but it was just dismissed as not going to happen. Politicians would never mention it because this would directly affect them and their overinflated salaries (once again, not going to happen). First, ladies and gentlemen, let me say that I believe that I'm a middle-of-the-road conservative, but I believe that liberals also have good ideas. I am *not* a Republican or a Democrat; I would consider that to be an insult to my intelligence. In fact, I strongly believe that this country needs at least four equally strong political parties for it to retain the greatness it was built upon. The two choices we now have every four years are usually pathetic. I myself seldom vote, as every four years, I feel like I'm watching a rerun of *Dumb and Dumber.* So what do we do with the economy? Well, I think the main problem with our economy is that it can no longer afford to pay our own salaries. Think about it (CEOs, Wall Street, politicians, Hollywood actors, lawyers, and many other people in America) making hundreds of thousands of dollars a year, then getting a million dollar bonus. There's no way these salaries can be justified. There's actually nothing a person can do that can justify this kind of pay. And who's paying these salaries? They didn't create something usable to justify their salaries (like a new source of energy). The cost of living went up to pay these salaries. So we're paying their salaries! This can actually be justified in only one way, so we shouldn't go around and just start shooting these people. However, I'm sure that people aren't aware of this justification, and if the people on the bottom were on the top, they would sadly do the same thing, so we're all equally at fault. Let me repeat that because it's very important! If the people on the bottom somehow got to the top, 99 percent of the time, they would probably do the same thing, so we're all equally at fault! In fact, a few years ago in an African nation, an army sergeant took over a country, and from what I heard, things got worse. Throughout history, I believe that on the few instances when the people on the bottom took over a country, things usually got worse instead of better. So we really can't be too upset with the people on the top because if we were up there, we would probably do the same thing. So what's the justification I mentioned earlier? For people accepting and feeling justified and completely comfortable in accepting these ridiculous salaries, and somehow feeling that they actually did something worth such ridiculous incomes, the justification is that it actually cost them their time! You see, God gives everyone just so much time, and it's not very long, and then you die. Our time here is finite. Death is our real destiny. So if we spend a large percentage (say 85 percent) of that time working, no amount of money can accurately compensate us for the time we gave to our jobs. You see, the most valuable thing we have is the time God gave us, and it's not very long. So if you give the majority of this time to your job (most people do), no amount of money can truly compensate a person for the time that he lost in his life. But now I believe that these high salaries are suffocating our economy. You know, ladies and gentlemen, we must be the ones paying for these salaries. There's just no way anyone can do anything that I can think of that's worth that much money (except if someone finally invented an alternate energy source that was 100 percent efficient in every way, shape, and form). That's really the only thing I can think of that would be worth that much money for the American people to pay. You may say, "How are the American people paying for this?" Well, there's nothing these people can do in my opinion that can possibly be worth this much money, so to pay their overinflated salaries, the cost of living must go up; that means that everything we buy costs more (food, heating oil, gas, etc.). An example of this would be that car mechanics now often charge one hundred dollars an hour; a loaf of bread can be almost four dollars at times. I think this all goes back to the fact that too many people in America get paid too much money and our economy can no longer afford to support our own salaries. So what do we do? I say everyone in America that is working gets paid thirty thousand dollars to one hundred fifty thousand dollars a year; that's it. People, I have worked as a geophysicist, a geologist, an officer in the merchant marine, a crew member in the merchant marine, a car mechanic, and a substitute schoolteacher, and I'm telling you, no job is that much harder than another. There's just no way anyone can justify the differences in salaries paid to different Americans. Yes, I know that some jobs have more responsibilities, some jobs require more skills, and some jobs are more backbreaking work; yes, this is true, but at the end of the day, they all pretty much equally suck. These factors would still be taken into account, so not everyone would be able to get to one hundred fifty thousand dollars, but everyone would start at thirty thousand dollars, say, out of high school. If a person went to college, he would start at thirty thousand plus what a person out of high school would make with four years work experience if he was a success at his job. Raises would be up to your company and how they think you're doing, just like today. A master's degree and PhD just follow the same principle. People like doctors, who have lots of responsibilities and skills, would eventually go to the one-hundred-fifty-thousand-dollar bracket (if they're good). Lots of other people would never get that high. Now this couldn't be done overnight. It would probably take twenty to thirty years. Presently, people making less than one hundred fifty thousand dollars could work their way up or stay where they're at, and people making more than one hundred fifty thousand dollars, their pay would be frozen and maybe reduced by a small percentage every year. Then once these people who are overpaid get old and finally leave the workforce, we could stabilize our salaries to thirty thousand dollars to one hundred fifty thousand dollars per year, which would lower the cost of living for everyone. I believe this would significantly lower the cost of living in America, and people would be less stressed out and have more time to enjoy their lives again. To enjoy the freedom and liberity again that this country was founded upon. Very few people in America today seem to be enjoying those freedoms. They're too busy working. Some people might call this socialism. Well, I don't know if it is nor do I care. Obviously, what we're doing today isn't working that well. One of my cousins is an engineer who works for the government. His job has a maximum pay scale that he has reached; he is happy and content with it. I think all Americans can learn from this and should start thinking in this direction.

One more thing, ladies, this one's for you—alimony. Sorry, girls, it's not a pension plan. You're going to have to give it up. In probably 99 percent of all breakups, it's both partners' fault. So you girls really can't expect a lifelong pension because you got divorced. Let's be fair. Alimony for six years—that will give you enough time to go to school, get a degree, and start yourselves on a new job and get comfortable with it. If you choose not to go to school, that will give you six years to work for a business or learn a skill and get back on your feet. Of course, child support would be paid as it is today; when the kids get out of school or they're a certain age, then payment will be stopped. That's more than fair girls. I went out with a girl in China once. Her husband threw her out; she got nothing. She told me over there, if your husband gets sick of you, he can throw you out any time, no questions asked. Now I don't agree with that, but I don't agree with the system in America either. I sailed with a captain once; he was paying his ex-wife three thousand dollars a month for life. That's not alimony, ladies; that's a pension. There's no way you can justify that!

Above are just a few ideas that I think people in America must start thinking of if we're going to find a real economic solution in this country that will last. A four-day work week so Americans can enjoy their lives again, and a minimum and maximum salary of thirty thousand dollars to one hundred fifty thousand dollars per year for every American—something our economy can afford.

I'll give you an example of why these high salaries can no longer be justified and how people should start looking at them. There was a movie recently called the *Hurt Locker*. This was about an army sergeant in Iraq who put his life on the line every day defusing bombs. He was an expert in what he did, one of the best in the business. He probably only made about thirty thousand dollars per year, if that much. I don't really know what he made, but when I was a lance corporal in the Marine Corps, I got paid sixty dollars per week. The actor who made believe he was him in the movie probably made hundreds of thousands of dollars or, more likely, millions of dollars. Do you see the problem, ladies and gentlemen? Why would an actor, someone who's just making believe they're him, get paid more than the guy who actually did it? I heard the sergeant wanted half the actor's pay. I doubt if he got it, but of course, he was entitled to it! He actually did it; he put his life on the line every day; he saved other people's lives. The actor just made believe he did it. How and why would the actor get paid more than the guy that actually did it? Come on, ladies and gentlemen, you have to be able to see this. You can and must take this example and use it throughout our entire society, from the White House to Wall Street to Hollywood to big and small businesses to lawyers, etc.

Another example I can think of is of a newsman who used to be a schoolteacher. Now a number of friends of mine have been teaching school for about thirty years. I'd say they make about seventy thousand dollars per year. Now the newsman, I would guess makes about six or seven figures per year. I heard that some sitcom actors in Hollywood make a couple of hundred thousand dollars per week per episode. I don't know if a newsman makes as much as a sitcom actor, but maybe he does. Anyway, I feel the newsman is one of the best in the business, but does he deserve to make that much more than he would have made if he remained a schoolteacher? Seventy thousand dollars per year compared to maybe up to a couple of hundred thousand dollars per week. I don't think so. I mean, why would he? Is telling the news more important than teaching America's youth? I don't think so. Is telling the news harder than teaching our youth? I don't think so. I'd say the hardest part of the job is research, and I believe that the network has their own research division, which does the bulk of that. So why would a newsman make that much more than a schoolteacher? And why in God's name would a Hollywood actor probably make a couple of million dollars when the person he's making believe he is only got about thirty thousand dollars for actually doing it. This is the problem, ladies and gentlemen, and you have to start seeing this. No one is really working all that much harder than anyone else. In our society, certain jobs pay lots more than others (this is a major problem). There's no way to really justify this, at least not to the extent to which it has grown to today. People started getting away with overcharging decades ago, if not longer, and it snowballed out of control. Once people found out they could get away with overcharging, they easily justified it within themselves, and once society sanctioned it, the cancer started to grow. This isn't good, ladies and gentlemen. It increases the cost of living for everyone. In the end, the middle class and the poor suffer for it. We indirectly get stuck paying for these ridiculously high salaries every time we have to buy something to continue living.

The point I'm trying to make, and a point that people must start to see, and recognize. Is that people who make 800,000 dollars a year , or 8 million dollars a year, or more then that a year, in general, aren't working any harder, nor are they any better at what they do, then most people who only make 70,000 dollars per year. I'll say that again because I think it's very important. Most people who make 800,000 dollars a year, or 8 million dollars a year, or more then that a year, in general, aren't working any harder, nor are they any better at what they do, then most people who make only 70,000 dollars per year. These salaries can no longer be justified, nor should our society continue to worship people who make these ridiculous salaries. Think about it!

Also, I think it's important to point out, that the maximum and minimum salaries I mentioned earlier (30,000 to 150,000 dollars per year) are the extreme. Thirty thousand dollars per year is fine for the minimum salary, but 150,000 dollars per year for the maximum is the extreme case. I started with 30,000 to 90,000 dollars per year as the maximum and minimum salaries. I think a maximum of 90,000 dollars per year, would be a foundational step that would eventually lower the cost of living, this would help solve all of America's economic problems. Now people keep charging more and more for their services which makes everything cost more. This drives the cost of living up. Soon no one will be able to afford to live here. However, peoples love of money in America, as well as the rest of the world, made me change the maximum amount first to 120,000 dollars per year, and then to 150,000 dollars per year. I feel that this is probably way too much. Remember that in most cases, no one is really working that much harder than anyone else, nor are they any better at what they do. If everyone in America got paid 30,000 to 90,000 dollars per year; I think it would be a huge foundational step in lowering the cost of living, which would help solve America's economic problems. And at this pay, people wouldn't be pushed so hard to always work too many hours, inadvertently enslaving themselves.

THE OTHER SIDE OF RACISM
(IT'S EMBARRASSING BEING WHITE, AND IT'S NOT ALL RIGHT TO BE LILY-WHITE)

RACISM—WELL, LADIES AND GENTLEMEN, WHERE do I begin? This part of the book I don't even want to write. Why? Because some black people will find it to be offensive, and most white people in America, Canada, and Europe won't have any idea what I'm talking about, nor will they even want to admit that this possibility exists. Most of these people will just label me a racist and not even try to understand what I'm saying. These are the people that make it possible for the other side of racism to exist. As for me, I don't believe I'm a racist; in fact, I usually get along better with black people than I do with white people. However, after reading this book, if you think I'm a racist, fine, I could care less. Another lesson lily-white people in America must learn.

However, this must be said: the time for ignorance and fear is over. There is another side to racism, and just being plain ignorant about its existence (as most white people are) doesn't make it OK. It seems to me that most black people know about this, but since it's been to their advantage, they're not saying anything about it; and most white people are completely unaware that another side to racism exists, which has been to their disadvantage. This situation has created a double standard in America, which I believe has created a foundational problem in the fabric of our culture. One that is so great and out of control, it may eventually destroy this nation. Once again, this does not apply to everyone and every situation, but people (especially white people) must see that there is another side to racism and start acting accordingly, or racism will never go away in this country. White people constantly play the fool every time a racial situation comes up, and are constantly running to the aid of whoever they think is being oppressed just to try so desperately hard to prove to the world that they're one of the good ones. This is no longer acceptable. Most black people will know what I'm talking about in this section of the book but won't want to say anything about it. It's more fun watching white people make complete fools out of themselves every time the word *racism* is mentioned by our media. This is also a form of racism (the other side of racism) and if people don't start acting accordingly, racism will never go away in this country. White people in America seem to be completely ignorant of the fact that black people can be racist too, or to the fact that this possibility even exists. Sorry, white people, but ignorance and fear is not an acceptable excuse in this day and age, and if you don't learn that there's another side to racism, it will never go away in America. In fact, most white people in this country won't even try to understand what I'm talking about. They've been too brainwashed by the media, and our culture, and present-day society since they've been born to see that there's another side to racism. It really is "embarrassing being white" these days. I've sailed around the world about fifteen times, got a master's degree in geophysics, and I served in the Marine Corps during the Vietnam War. From this experience and from what I've seen, I've come up with the conclusion that the white race is no more racist than any other race on the planet. However, in the media, whether it's books, TV, or newspapers, the white race is always depicted as the evil race that is responsible for all the world's racial problems. This is a bias which is just a polite way of saying the word *racism* in these situations. The real problem being that white people actually believe this and everyone else, on most occasions, is just laughing at their stupidity. I personally believe that racism and our country's love of money are probably the foundation of all America's social and cultural problems. And all this stupidity about being politically correct, which people in America have handcuffed themselves to, is probably the foundation of a host of problems, which may eventually destroy this nation.

So where do I start? This is a long and confusing story that also started in 1972 when I joined the United States Marine Corps. My parents, like most white parents, taught me nothing about racism. I believed and learned about racism from watching TV and reading books and magazine articles like most white people. Well, nothing could have been further from the truth. Books, like TV, from what I've found since my days in the corps, can be and usually are very, very biased against white people when it comes to this subject, and bias in general on most other topics.

An example of this happened to me when I was younger. I used to love to read books about the early American West, especially about the era of the mountain men. On one occasion, I read two books about the Indian wars dealing with Custer's Last Stand. After reading one book, you thought every white man was the biggest piece of crap on the planet, and that we owed the Indians everything, and should constantly go out of our way to always be extra nice to them. Likewise, after reading the second book, you were left with the opinion that you should go out and kill every Indian you ever meet. So what's the difference? How could this be? Two different books about the same historical fact; I mean Custer's Last Stand did happen right? So why would two different books about the same historical event leave a reader with two completely different reactions. Why? Because one book was total bias against white people and one book was total bias against Indians. Likewise, in present-day America, probably 98 percent of all books and TV and any media coverage is totally biased against white people when it comes to the topic of racism, often leaving you feeling that white people owe black people everything and that they should feel obligated to go out of their way to be extra nice to them. This is not good, ladies and gentlemen. This doesn't end racism; it just prolongs it and points it in a different direction.

I remember my first night in the Marine Corps after training ended. About six black guys came into our barracks about 2:00 a.m. and beat the hell out of some white guy who was asleep just because his skin was white. At the time, I was thinking, *How could this be?* Can TV be wrong? Can books be wrong? According to our media, it's always white people doing this to black people, not the opposite. Well, by the time my tour in the corps was completed, I came to the undeniable conclusion that, yes, American media, whether it's books, TV, or magazines, is usually the complete opposite of the truth when it comes to the topic of racism in America. During my time in the corps, I'm sad to say, that a large percentage of the black marines I served with were just the biggest bunch of racist pigs you'd ever want to meet. Always saying how the black race was the master race and how they were superior to white people. I couldn't believe it. According to books and TV, white people always talked like that, but to tell you the truth, I don't ever remember hearing white people actually saying things like that except on TV. So was it true? I've come to the conclusion that it wasn't. Sadly, this is how white people usually learn about racism—from watching TV or reading books. Of course, lots of black marines I served with did an excellent job, and I became good friends with many of them. However, the racist pigs ruled the day back then. Black power signs were everywhere on base; it was disgraceful. This completely destroyed a large part of discipline in the Marine Corps when I served, and, I believe, was a major factor in the pathetic results we achieved in Vietnam (a peace agreement that only lasted two years). In general, I would sadly say that desegregation was a complete failure in the military during the Vietnam War. This policy resulted in a big breakdown in military discipline and a major reason for our pathetic results in our attempt to fight the war.

So people, especially white people, have to learn not to believe everything they read or see on TV. After all, authors can be very biased (not even knowing it) and the people in Hollywood often are only interested in making pictures that sell (with little regard for the truth). If you think about it, probably 98 percent of the people writing these books never had to live through any bad racial problems in their lives, so what would they really know? And the rich lily-white people in Hollywood that control the biggest part of the media (TV) what are the chances of them really knowing anything about racism? It's slim at best. Believe me, ladies and gentlemen (especially white people) if you've never been in a bad racial situation, you don't know anything about racism. And the majority of white people in America and the rest of the world (especially you lily-white people who control the media), it's very obvious in most situations that you've never been in a bad racial situation. Making you unqualified in any way, shape, or form to write books about it, teach it in our schools (multiculturalism), or make movies or TV programs with its contents within it, or report it on the news! At this point, many white people in America will say, "What about slavery?" Don't worry about slavery if it's preventing you from seeing the bigger picture. Slavery was a worldwide epidemic years ago; even white people were slaves. In the days of the Roman Empire, if a person couldn't pay their bills, it was not uncommon for him and his family to be sold as slaves. In early America, Indian tribes would fight wars and enslave their captives. During the Lewis and Clark Expedition, two Indian women saved the lives of Lewis and Clark and the entire expedition on two separate occasions. Both were former slaves who escaped their slavery and made it back to their own tribe. Both of these women came to the aid of Lewis and Clark when their tribe planned on killing them. These women both told their tribe how white people had been kind to them and helped them escape the cruelty of their slavery. In both instances, the tribe spared the lives of Lewis and Clark due to the white man's kind treatment to these women (from the documentary *Undaunted Courage*).

How come white people never hear about this in the media? Why not? I was working in Africa a few years back (in Liberia). When we got to the country, we were given about a thirty-page paper about the country including its history. I was surprised to read that after the Civil War, some American blacks were returned to Liberia, at which time, they enslaved the black Africans there. How could this be? I never heard or saw that in the American media, which pretty much dictates and controls the way people think in America, Europe, and Canada on the topic of racism. I myself have been to Africa on thirty different occasions to twenty different countries (Djibouti, Eritrea, Gambia, Ghana, Guinea, Algeria, Angola, Benin, Cameroon, Congo, Ivory Coast, Egypt, Kenya, South Africa, Liberia, Sierra Leone, Somalia, Tanzania, Mozambique, and Mauritania) and, in general, found the African people to be very nice, and I enjoyed my stay every time. However, the poverty over there is depressing as it is in most third world countries, and I believe that lots of Africans today would gladly come to America as slaves for a period of time, say two years, if they were promised their freedom after this period. I think that in some African countries, the people over there would probably end up killing each other to get on these ships and come to America to be slaves for a short period of time before they were freed. Am I saying that this is a good idea? *Hell no!* Do I think we should do this? *Hell no!* I'm saying this because white people have to learn the truth. Slavery was a worldwide epidemic throughout most of world history. Native Americans commonly enslaved captives of other tribes in early America. Why don't we ever hear about this? White people have to stop feeling guilty, sorry, afraid, or obligated to black people in America and stop running to their defense every time something comes up that may be racist. They're just making complete fools out of themselves every time the topic of racism comes up, and it's really getting to be embarrassing. More importantly, this kind of stupid behavior won't end racism in America.

Now remember, people (white, black, red, or yellow), this does not apply to everyone and every situation, but it applies enough that people (especially white people) need to become aware of it. If not, racism will never go away in this country!

I'll give you some examples. The list of examples can go on and on; all anyone really has to do is watch the news at night, or read the newspaper, and it won't take long before you see examples for yourselves of what I'm talking about. You just have to keep your eyes open and forget what you've been brainwashed to believe by our society and media since you've been born. Can you do this? Most people can't.

Of course, you'll never hear anything like these examples in all that politically correct baloney, and multicultural propaganda, that our schools are presently brainwashing our children with these days.

One example I can give is when I went to college for two years in the state of Montana. Once during this time, a teacher told me that the school had people from the East come from the board of education to inspect the school's curriculum. I was told that these people said or cared nothing about reading, writing, math, science, computers, engineering, or anything else the school had to offer. The only thing they cared or talked about was multiculturalism; and was the school thoroughly brainwashing the kids with this. Not one word about math and science, computers, and all the rest of the stuff that is the foundation of education worldwide. The scariest part is that this teacher (a white woman) was glad and ecstatic to tell the class of this important meeting and how multiculturalism was the topic of the day; in fact, the only topic of the day. It wasn't until a few weeks later when I had a chance to point out to her that if people from the board of education from the East came all the way out here to talk about the school's curriculum, and all they talked about was multiculturalism, and how more of this subject was needed in the school, that this was just a form of racism (the other side of racism). Then the lightbulb went on in her head, and she realized something might not be right. However, she had a PhD—why didn't she figure this out for herself? White people never figure this out; they've been completely brainwashed by our culture and media while they're growing up that it's always the white man who's a racist pig.

Now I realize that white people are racist pigs at times, but this is well documented by the media, so I'm not going to be redundant and repeat all that, nor do I think this is acceptable. I'm not writing this book to put black people down, and I apologize to black people if they take it that way. I'm writing this book because white people have to learn that there's another side to racism and start acting accordingly, or racism will never go away in the world. And I'm *not* saying to white people to go out and join some kind of stupid hate group. In fact, when I work on cargo ships, often many of the people onboard are black, and I often get along better with them than most of the white people on board. Believe me, if you've never been in a bad racial situation you don't know what racism is!

Another example would be my first night in the Marine Corps after training I mentioned earlier. They beat the hell out of this guy just because his skin was white. In the early 1970s, to my surprise and disbelief, it was the black people in the Marine Corps that were the racist pigs, not the white people. Throughout my tour, I heard them saying constantly how they were the master race and how they were superior to white people; it was pathetic. It was pure racism (the other side of racism), the part white people better start seeing, or racism will never go away in this country. Ignorance won't make it disappear, and acting like fools doesn't work. How could this be possible? Everything white people are taught from birth is that we're the racist pigs and that we should be extra nice to black people every chance we get to atone for the sins of the past. Big mistake, white people. This doesn't solve the problem of racism; it just points it in a different direction.

Another example would be Professor Gates and the white cop situation a few years ago up in the Boston area. Do you remember Professor Gates of Harvard University (a black guy) who was trying to get back into his house (apparently he locked himself out) when a concerned neighbor called the police. A white cop came and confronted the professor and a confrontation occurred. Exactly what happened is unclear but the real problem occurred when the word *racism* echoed through the media. Now the point I'm trying to make and that people in America must come to understand is that racism charges in the media and our society were only mentioned against the white cop. Why? There's a 50 percent possibility that if racism was a factor, that Professor Gates could have been the racist. Is Professor Gates a racist? I don't know nor do I care, but the media and white America not even being aware that this possibility exists is a form of racism (the other side of racism). This uneducated approach to solving racial problems is very biased (which is racism in itself) and is never ending in America, Europe, and Canada. This ignorance by white people helps keep racism alive and well in the world today.

Another example—now I know that some interracial couples are legitimate, and I apologize to them for this, but this must be said. When I was in the Marine Corps, more than half of my unit was black, and every time a black guy would be with a white girl for the next month and a half, all you would hear was "I was fucking a white bitch. I was fucking a white bitch." All the black guys would be laughing and bragging about it. This is racism, ladies and gentlemen (the other side of racism). Come on, white people, even you can see this. White girls seem to be completely unaware of this as I was before I joined the Marine Corps, and the brothers taught me what was really going on. Another good example of this would be when I was working on a cargo ship with two good friends of mine that were both black. They were on deck talking about girls one day when I heard one of them say to the other one, "You know a lot of white girls will let us fuck them just because our skin is black. At first I thought, Eew, this is weird, but now I fuck all those white bitches." Then they both started laughing. Well, that's racism, ladies and gentlemen (the other side of racism). But the real problem is that white girls constantly whore themselves with black guys, trying so desperately hard to prove that "they're one of the good ones." I can remember the brothers in the Marine Corps constantly saying this as they were laughing at them. White girls who do this, you know who you are. Believe me, you're not being one of the good ones or forming some kind of special bond, which you're trying so desperately hard to do. You're just being fucked and laughed at. Back to the Marine Corps, another of the brother's favorite jokes was to badger a white girl being very, very persistent until they got what they wanted. They knew the white girl was scared to say no to them, fearing that this may be perceived as racism, so often being very persistent, asking them to dance or a date, they intentionally made them feel uncomfortable then come out with their famous line, "You're not prejudiced, are you?" Well, at this point, the poor white girl was completely frozen to her very core, kinda looking like a deer caught in a car's headlights. Then you'd hear the brothers all laughing and the one telling the story saying, "Next thing I know, I'm fucking this white bitch. I'm fucking this white bitch." Well, white girls, you can shoot down a white guy with no trouble; if you can't do the same to a guy whose skin happens to be black, you're in real danger of being manipulated, fucked, and laughed at. I suggest you go back to the basics. You don't need to explain yourself to any guy, and if you feel you need to because a guy's skin is black, you need to actually explain yourself even less. This again is an example of the other side of racism. If you're at this point, girls, go back to the basics; don't even try to explain yourself. You're a girl remember. Just say yes, no, I gotta go, just like you're talking to a white guy. Anything more than this shows your ignorance of racism and that's what they're looking for to make a fool out of you. Once again, I apologize to real interracial couples, but from what I've seen, this is a small percentage of the time.

Another example—an Ivy League school and the Black Panthers. This is a good one, ladies and gentlemen. Please try to understand what I'm talking about. A member of my family went to an Ivy League school, which I'm sure is a very good school, but I fear they're brainwashing the kids there with all this political correctness and multicultural propaganda. Don't be surprised. This is standard curriculum at all schools in America these days. To prove my point, I was up there one weekend and was informed that one of the vice presidents of the Black Panthers was coming on campus to give a lecture. Once again, I'm not surprised that a lily-white school in America would do this. After all, the chances of college professors with PhDs in America knowing anything about what racism really is, is slim (remember, if you've never been in a bad racial situation, you probably don't know anything about racism). I would guess maybe as high as 99 percent of teachers in America have never been in a bad racial situation, making them unqualified to teach it. However, this next example is very straightforward even white people should be able to figure this one out. Now I don't really care about the school letting the Black Panthers on the campus. What I do care about is the fact that this lily-white school would probably never in a million years let the KKK on their campus, and I support them for that. However, I'm sure that if people think about it, many or most people would come up with the very real possibility that the KKK and the Black Panthers are just the opposite sides of the same coin. Not only that, but most of the lily-white students at the school, I would venture to say, actually got to the auditorium hours early to get a good seat for the Black Panthers. Now—and this is the important part, folks, so pay attention—if the KKK was asked to speak at this school, these same students wouldn't show up early to get a good seat; they would probably hold demonstrations outside the auditorium trying to stop the speech, which they probably should do, but these same lily-white students should have also showed up early to stop the Black Panthers from speaking on campus. Instead, they roll out the red carpet and arrived early to get a good seat. How stupid is that, ladies and gentlemen? And would these same lily-white students have showed up early or at all if this event was held outside a school in a black neighborhood, say, like Rutgers University in Camden, New Jersey? And if they did show up, would things have been the same? And that's the other side of racism—the point I'm trying to get across to Americans. You can't have double standards in this country when it comes to racism, and that's what we have today in America. Racism will never go away in this country as long as there are double standards. The lily-white students at the school would have demonstrated and maybe even got violent if the KKK was asked to speak at their school, but when the Black Panthers come, they throw out the welcome mat and show up early to get a good seat. That's the other side of racism, ladies and gentlemen, and if you don't understand what I'm talking about, there's no hope for this country. Our schools are doing such a thorough job of brainwashing our kids with being politically correct and multiculturalism these days that even the most powerful job in the whole world was directly affected by it in our last election. Now

I don't know if Barack Obama will be a good president or not, and at this point, I don't care. What I do care about is that millions and millions and millions and millions of white people voted for Barack Obama because his skin is half black. Barack Obama was elected because he got the white vote, not because he got the black vote or any other vote. The only mention I heard of this on the news was by the black news commentator, Juan Williams, on Fox News. He said this one night on the Bill O'Reilly show, "Barack Obama is going to be the next president of the United States because his skin is black." I couldn't believe it. Bill O'Reilly, who calls his show "the no spin zone," completely spun out of it that night. He just started talking about something else as if Juan Williams hadn't said anything. Now I think that Bill O'Reilly is one of the best newsmen on TV, and I was shocked that he didn't understand the importance of what Juan said or just felt too uncomfortable to speak about the subject. Millions and millions and millions and millions of white people voted for Barack Obama because his skin is half black. How do I know this? Because before I went into the Marine Corps and the brothers taught me different, I would have voted for Obama. I would have felt (I don't know the right word) compelled, obligated, obsessed, etc. to put Obama in the White House because his skin is half black, feeling I was waving my freedom flag high for all black people to see. Come on, white people, how many of you voted for him for this reason? Come on; admit it. Just look at the stupid behavior of Europeans before the election. When Obama visited Europe before the election, millions and millions of white people showed up to show their undying support for a black man running for the presidency. Let's face it, and finally admit to ourselves that if Obama's skin was all white instead of half white, less than one-quarter of these people would have showed up. That's a double standard or racism, ladies and gentlemen, the other side of racism, the side that white people don't see and don't want to see. Face it, ladies and gentlemen. That's a double standard, and if white people don't get rid of this double standard, racism will never go away in this country. Do you realize that Barack Obama received 95 percent of the black vote during the election? By the way, I only heard this reported on Fox News; maybe I just missed it everywhere else. Now if John McCain received 95 percent of the white vote, the word *racism* would have been plastered on the front page of almost every newspaper in America. But when Obama gets 95 percent of the black vote, there's no real mention of it. Once again, that's racism, ladies and gentlemen, the other side of racism. Europe and Canada are even worse and more stupid when it comes to racism. Usually, the only examples of racism they have to learn from are American television (they're really doomed)!

Moving along to the election—now I realize that with the near collapse of our entire economic system because of the Republicans' continued insistence that because of the free-market system that our country and our economy never needs any government help, it will automatically repair itself (obviously this is wrong because almost every time the Republicans get into office, the middle class and the poor suffer economically in this country). But even way before the economic disaster of 2008, I seemed to be one of the very few white people in the world that knew that Obama would be the next president mostly due to the fact that his skin is half black, and Juan Williams, a black man, was the only news commentator who even tried to bring this to the attention of the American people. Of course, the rest of the media completely missed the importance of what Juan said or where too afraid to address the topic. Even Bill O'Reilly completely bombed that night when he completely, and I believe intentionally, ignored what Juan said that night. OK, with that stated, let's look at some disturbing facts in the election that white people in America completely missed. It really is embarrassing being white, and if you read this article, you should be able to see just how stupid white people are when it comes to racism.

Number one is the Reverend Wright thing. Now I don't know if Reverend Wright is a racist or not nor do I care; but what I do care about is the fact that if Joe Biden, John McCain, or Sarah Palin went to a church for twenty-two years where a white minister was preaching and saying racist things against black people, and hateful things against America, with racism always looming in the background, all three of them would have been thrown out of the election immediately (two weeks tops and they would have been sent home crying like little babies). Obama got a complete pass. In fact, most white people, probably the stupidest people on the whole planet when it comes to racism; we're not even aware of this. If you did mention it, they would just smile and say, "Oh, that doesn't bother me," like they're one of the good ones, or they'd say, "Yeah, I know," acknowledging what happened and admitting it bothered them, but this had no real effect on the way they acted or voted. If one of the three white people (Biden, McCain, or Palin) did this, these very same white people would have demanded their immediate dismissal from the campaign. This is racism (the other side of racism), and if you don't start seeing it, white people, racism will never go away in America. It's a double standard; the same laws that apply to white people must also apply to black people or racism will never go away in this country. I can still hear the brothers laughing in the Marine Corps when white people said this. Well, ladies and gentlemen, this has to bother you because it's racism (the other side of racism). White people, you can't have a double standard in this country when it comes to racism. The same rules that apply to white people must also apply to black people. If this doesn't happen, then racism will never go away in this country, and this has to bother you. You're not being one of the good ones; you're just making complete fools out of yourselves. And if you're doing this because you're afraid, then shame on you. Mr. President, I ask that you don't run in 2012 due to the Reverend Wright thing for the reasons I mentioned above. Now most white people are completely confused at this point, but since you're half black, you know exactly what I'm talking about. I ask that you don't run in 2012. Sorry, black people, but most of you were completely aware of this and said nothing, so most of you are also guilty of racism too (the other side of racism). Juan Williams, was the only black person I know of who mentioned this, and the only news man in all America to see this and had the courage to state it. Of course, white people completely missed the importance of what he said.

Another example of racism during the election (the other side of racism) is when the media kept saying that the affluent young white people were voting for Obama. What does that mean? If you're not voting for Obama, you're an ignorant, worthless piece of shit, possibly a racist? That's a racist statement! And why where the young white kids so heavily supportive of Obama? Could it be that these kids had been so thoroughly brainwashed in our schools with being politically correct and multiculturalism that they where inwardly terrified at voting against him? Inwardly being made to feel that they now were playing an important part in righting all the wrongs of the past, something they know nothing about? Being made to feel, after years of propaganda, by our schools and the media, that they finally got their chance to wave their freedom flags high. How do I know this? Because before I joined the Marine Corps and the brothers taught me different, I would've voted for Obama for the same reasons. Well, lily-white people, I can still hear the brothers laughing in the Marine Corps and bragging about how they were going to take over the country and white people were so stupid they didn't even realize this was happening. Sorry, black people, I don't mean this to be offensive. I have nothing against black people, but if white people don't see that there's another side to racism and start acting accordingly, racism will never go away in this country. I really think that present-day racism, and the "stupidity of making money" in this country, is probably the foundation of all America's social and cultural problems. And I don't mean that in a biased way. I have nothing against white people or black people, but if people in America (especially white people) don't realize that there's another side to racism and start acting accordingly it will never go away in this country.

You may have noticed that I'm always putting down being politically correct and multiculturalism. Why? Because in many instances, being politically correct has literally handcuffed our nation. Nothing can ever be said to anyone or any group of people in this country anymore if it may seem negative. This stupid behavior has had a disastrous effect on our country's ability to deal effectively with our own internal problems. Hey, let's face it. Both white, black, red, and yellow there are alot of good people out there, but there're also some real idiots, and sometimes the best thing to do is just state this—something the media seems incapable of doing in this day and age when it comes to the topic of racism. Always stick with the truth, ladies and gentlemen, especially you guys in the media. In the long run, you'll always be ahead. Plus, people in America, whether you're white, black, red, or yellow, must absolutely and must finally understand that what you read in books and magazines or hear on TV 96 percent of the time has some bias attached to it. It's imperative that you understand this, or once again, racism and many other problems will never go away in this country. Books and magazines aren't the bible, and most of the people who work on TV probably aren't any smarter than you are. So why constantly act as if they are? Most people that write books or report the news want you to see things the way they see it (this is a bias). You have to be able to sort through this information and pick out the truth, realizing that internally you have your own biases, which you must try to keep in check as best you can to structure the truth. Not an easy job for anyone and a job the media has failed terribly in, on the topic of racism, as well as many other topics in the world today. And then there's multiculturalism. In many ways, from what I've seen, this has been created to make white people feel guilty, and obligated. So is this really multiculturalism or racism (the other side of racism)? From what I've seen, it's probably just racism. I'll give you an example: Black History Month.

I mean, what is this? Where did they get this from? Who's the idiot that thought of this? Is this multiculturalism or racism (the other side of racism)? The side of racism people in America better start seeing if they want racism to go away in this country. I mean, why isn't there a Native American History Month or a Latino History Month or an Oriental History Month or a White History Month? So is multiculturalism really multiculturalism, or is it black culturalism? I mean, why should black people get more recognition than Native Americans or Latinos or Orientals or Whites? Isn't this racism? I think so. Think of it. I mean, Native Americans owned this country before the rest of us came over here and took it from them. So why in multiculturalism do they get much less recognition than black people? Is it because of slavery? So what! Who cares! Hey, white people, you have got to get over this, or racism will never go away in this country. Like I explained earlier, slavery was a worldwide epidemic years ago; even white people were slaves. I've been to Africa thirty different times. Pretty much every black person I ever met over there's biggest dream is to come to America. Why would this be, if White Americans are the bunch of racist pigs that books, newspapers, magazines, and TV depict us to be? Why would they all want to come here? Dah! Think about it. So why is there a Black History Month and not a Native American History Month or a Latino History Month or an Oriental History Month or a White History Month? And more importantly, do I think we should make a Native American or Latino or Oriental or White history month? *Hell no!* History is history; just teach real history (the truth) in our schools and society and get rid of all this bias. Remember, bias is just another way of saying the word *racism*. Once again,

I'm sorry, black people, if this offends some of you, but if white people don't start seeing this, racism will never go away in this country. Black people, once again, you are also responsible for this problem. Most of you know what I'm talking about and have done nothing to correct it. I was working with a black person recently who stated to me that she thought blacks from Africa and Central America kinda looked down on African Americans. The reasoning was on grounds of racism. She stated, "We're all black, so there shouldn't be any friction between us." Well, this is racism, ladies and gentlemen, the other side of racism. African Americans are the only people I met in all my travels around the world who know what color they are and who make race such a big issue. White Americans don't know they're white. Africans don't know they're black. Europeans don't know they're white. South Americans don't know if they're white, black, or Latino. Only black Americans seem to know what color they are, and from what I've seen, they want to keep it that way. Now, people, if you could look up this behavior in the dictionary, that would probably be the definition of *racism*. The rest of the world, or the people who don't know what color they are, if you could look that up in the dictionary, that would probably be the definition of not being a racist. The truth is, for racism to go away in this country, everybody has to start treating everyone else as individuals, not white people or black people or Latinos or Orientals or Native Americans. Do you think you can do this? Right now, I think we still have a ways to go, and if people (especially white people) don't learn that there's another side to racism and quit playing the fool every time the topic of racism comes up in America, it will never go away.

Once again, this book obviously does not apply to every situation and racial circumstance in America, and this part of the book in no way justifies stupid people to go out and join some kind of ridiculous hate group. This is just to inform people (especially white people) that there is another side to racism, and not being aware of it or making believe that it doesn't exist is just plain stupid. Now there's nothing wrong with any race—white, black, red, or yellow—but all people must start seeing the incredible amount of bias in the American media, usually against white people, when it comes to race. Whether it's books, TV, newspapers, or magazines, this bias is usually there. Until this bias goes away, racism will never go away in the world.

I personally think the third part of my book, "The Other Side of Racism," should be required reading at every school in America where political correctness and multiculturalism is preached. Why? Because they're only teaching the kids half the story; this is a brief introduction to the other half. Remember, you need to know both sides of every story to get to the truth.

CONCLUSION

WELL PEOPLE, I'M SORRY, I know that what I said was a bit condescending at times; but after watching our country make the same mistakes over and over again for about thirty five years, I felt something had to be said. The statements in this book do not apply to every situation and circumstance that our nation faces. However, they do apply enough that I think people in America should start to think in this direction when the circumstance's warrant it.

Well, there's good and bad. I've traveled around the world many, many times, and the good news is whether you're white or black, rich or poor, liberal or conservative, industrialized world or third world, I see hope everywhere in individuals. The bad news is I believe our society, economy, political system, and media are seriously broken and may not be repairable. It all started during the Vietnam War when people in America found out just how stupid and impotent our politicians were. Before this, we believed they were honest, trustworthy, and intelligent; and of course, the cowards of the peace movement during the war, who spit on the American military. This was the first time in our nation's history that a generation of Americans spit on the American military and ran from a confrontation. These very same people are running the country now, so what would you expect? Well, hopefully we can keep the status quo, but I got my doubts.

The good news is, in all my travels around the world, I see hope everywhere in individuals. The bad news is, governments and some of the media, are so out of touch with reality and common everyday people that things may be broken beyond repair. Personally, I think God is the only one who can solve the world's problems. His solution was his son, but the world ignored that solution and always will, but that's OK. I personally don't believe Christ came to save the world. I think he came to save individuals. Why? Because he knew trying to save the world would be a waste of time.